The Royal Canadian Legion

1926–1986

The Royal Canadian Legion

1926–1986

Photographs / Jack Jarvie
Text / Diana Swift

Discovery Books

Produced for The Royal Canadian Legion
by Discovery Books
70 The Esplanade
Toronto, Ontario
Canada, M5E 1R2

Designed by Newton Frank
Printed in Hong Kong by Everbest Printing Co., Ltd.

PHOTO CREDITS

Unless otherwise indicated, black and white archival photos are from the files of The Royal Canadian Legion, Ottawa.

York University Archives, *Toronto Telegram* Collection, Toronto:
Arthur Currie, p. 16, DND; Canadians at Mons, p. 17, DND.

Public Archives of Canada, Ottawa:
Canadian soldiers entering war-torn Caen, p. 13, top left, H.C. Aikman, DND, PA 363295; Canadian troops at Durban, p. 15, PA 16388; Billy Bishop, p. 16, PA 1654; naval commandos, p. 18, R.G. Arless, DND, PA 136281; German prisoners, p. 19, F.L. Dubervill, DND, PA 136280; Canadian privates, Korea, p. 19, W.H. Olson, DND, PA 128869; Vimy surrender, p. 22, PA 1123; GWVA, p. 22, PA 138949; Lord Byng, p. 23, PA C-39555.

This book is dedicated to
the 600,000 men and women of
The Royal Canadian Legion.

A piper marches past the National War Memorial in Ottawa on Remembrance Day, November 11, 1984.

Foreword

This story, in words and pictures, recounts the dedication of men and women to The Royal Canadian Legion and to Canada. The recognition here is primarily of the organization rather than of the many individuals who, in the branches and at provincial and Dominion commands, deserve so much credit.

We lived through an important period of history when Canadians responded to the call to arms and served bravely to defend the cause of freedom. The book tells of the efforts of the Legion to ensure that the proper needs of the veterans and their dependants were and continue to be met and, accompanying that duty, the consequent movement of the Legion into general community service.

You are invited to share with us in this unique story of how those who served have created a legacy of patriotism and social responsibility, which they are determined to pass on to their successors.

His Honour Alfred Watts, AFC, ED, QC
Grand President
The Royal Canadian Legion
Vancouver, April 1985

Contents

World War I soldiers lend support to a wounded comrade in the field.

PART ONE
LOOKING BACK

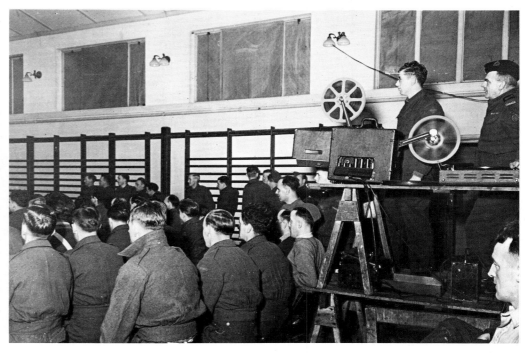

1 Citizen Soldiers

The figure of the citizen soldier is as old as human civilization. Throughout history, ordinary people, overtaken by war, have dropped their peacetime pursuits and willingly taken up arms in defence of their countries. At hostilities' end, they have returned to blend back into the communities they left to defend. This was true in ancient Egypt, classical Greece and Rome, and mediaeval Europe; and it has been equally true of a country as young as Canada.

Though sparsely populated and possessing no substantial standing armies, this country contributed contingents of largely volunteer soldiers to several foreign conflicts: the South African War, 1899–1902; World War I, 1914–18; World War II, 1939–45; and the Korean War, 1950–53. Many servicemen lost their lives and many more suffered in body and spirit, but most returned from the crucible of military duty to add a new and tempered vitality to communities galvanized — and often transformed — by war.

On our behalf, these citizen soldiers saw and suffered things that no one should have to. And, indeed, Canadian veterans have been determined to spare their children and grandchildren similar hardships. But if our veterans have striven to avoid any recurrence of the horrors of world war, they have also

Having helped Britain to victory against the Boers, some of the 7,000 Canadian soldiers raised for the South African War embark at Durban in 1902 for the long voyage home.

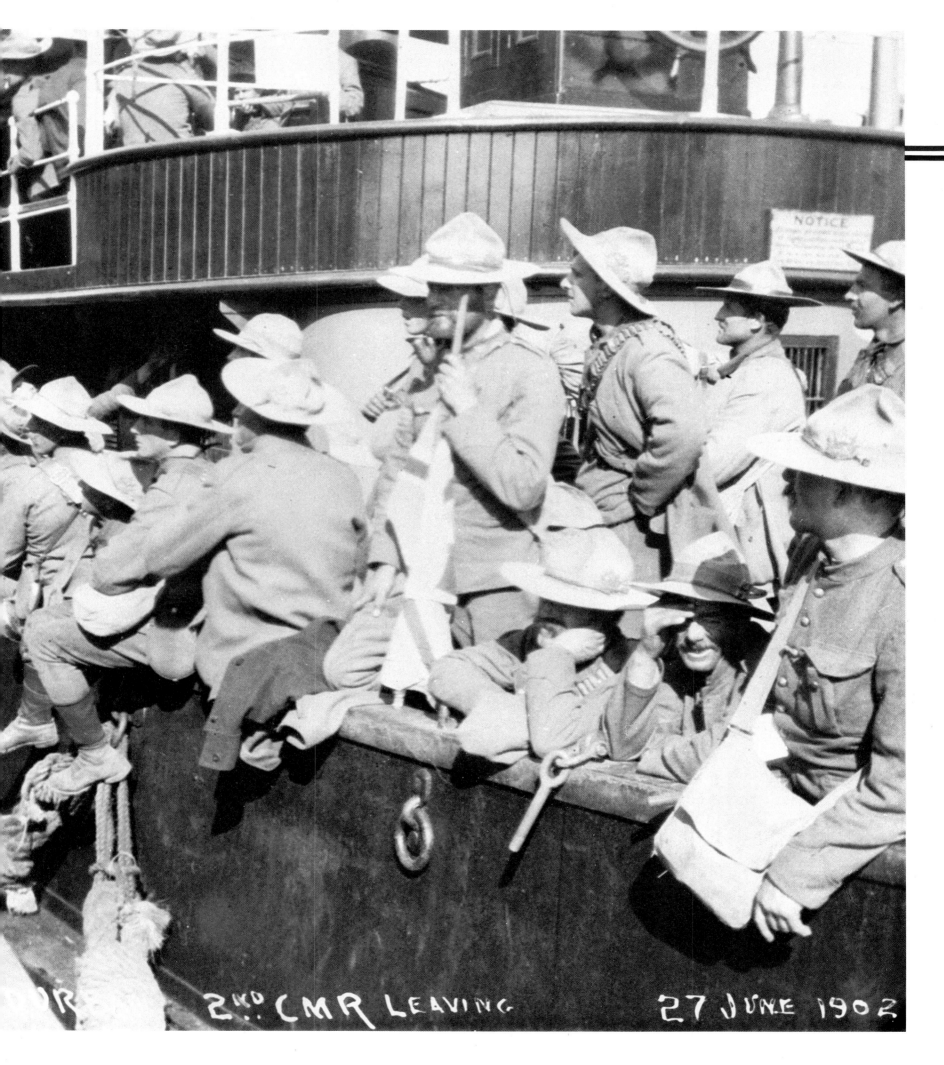

2ND CMR LEAVING   27 JUNE 1902

Lieutenant-General Sir Arthur Currie, the classic Canadian citizen soldier. A Victoria businessman and militia volunteer, Currie quickly rose to become commander of the Canadian Corps in World War I, leading them with particular distinction in the decisive battle of Amiens in 1918. Later, he served as president of the Canadian Legion, 1928–29.

Lieutenant-Colonel William Avery ''Billy'' Bishop, Canada's most dashing knight of the air in the Great War. As a top ace with Britain's Royal Flying Corps, Bishop downed 72 enemy planes and won a Victoria Cross for a solo attack on a German airfield in France.

A candid camera caught these Canadian soldiers in a happy mood in November 1918 after the liberation of the Belgian town of Mons — where the British first engaged the Germans in August 1914 — brought hostilities to an end.

maintained a healthy respect for the qualities that made for such dedicated soldiering. They have continued to salute the exacting discipline of military training and active service that both hardened their mettle and heightened their awareness of the needs of their comrades.

The strengths forged in the field could not be casually laid aside in peacetime. And Canadian society has benefited from the fusion of veterans' ideals with our collective national consciousness, ideals that have influenced business, industry, education, and government. But if one wishes to see those ideals at work in greater relief than can be seen in society as a whole, one must look to The Royal Canadian Legion. It is a repository of the values of our citizen soldiers writ large.

Today the Legion is an organization of large numbers, substantial wealth, and great influence. Not all of its 600,000 members are veterans; and as the veteran population ages with the approach of the 21st century, it is clear the Legion will have to broaden its base still further. Otherwise it cannot maintain its current strength to carry on the work it was founded to do. But that notwithstanding, the veteran and his values will remain the central hub of the Legion wheel that must radiate out through many spokes to touch a circumference larger than itself.

As the pages of this Jubilee book will show, The Royal Canadian Legion enjoys an outstanding record of community service, legislative progressiveness, and national consciousness-raising. And, for the most part, it has carried on this work in the same volunteering spirit that has set Canadian soldiers apart from the military personnel of other lands. The Legion the reader will meet in these pages is a body dedicated to discipline, excellence, and the welfare of its own and other people. But while it believes in helping others, it also believes in self-help, sharing Abraham Lincoln's conviction that one must not do for others what they can and should do for themselves.

Throughout its hundreds of branches, as diverse and wide-ranging as Canada itself, the Legion fosters close ties of comradeship through social activities and social services. It is intimately involved in medical charity and research, enlightened building programmes, and the welfare of the young and the elderly. It has striven to promote the generous treatment of ex-servicemen and women and their

D-Day, June 6, 1944: the first German prisoners taken by Canadian soldiers are guarded on the Normandy beachhead.

Opposite: An integrated group of young naval commandos, including some Canadians, on exercises off the coast of England about a month before D-Day. *Above:* Two Canadian privates stand guard over the Imjin River, North Korea, in 1951. Some 25,000 Canadians served under the United Nations flag in the Korean War.

dependants. In all this it displays a modest, unsung, and low-key persona. Only in honouring the memory of those fallen or broken in the service of their country does it step forward and assume a higher profile.

The Legion has never broken faith with those who fell, and its works remain a living monument to them. It continues to remind Canadians that they must remember both the sacrifice and the concept of freedom for which it was made. In this the Legion has been our national conscience.

Back in the first century B.C., the great Roman poet Horace wrote one of the most famous lines in Western literature:

Exegi monumentum aere perennius
I have built a memorial more lasting
than bronze.

Horace was speaking of the immortality of his own lyric poetry. Yet the line seems equally appropriate to the active body of tribute formed by the dedicated membership of The Royal Canadian Legion. The commitment of its comrades past and present, and of the new people who stand poised to receive its colours and carry them forward into the 21st century, is far more significant than the most revered of inanimate memorials. For it constitutes a living and unbroken gesture of acknowledgment and thanks. And a more enduring monument than that, no fallen soldier could ever have.

2 Beginnings

It was with innocent optimism that Prime Minister Sir Wilfrid Laurier declared, in 1904, that the 20th century belonged to Canada. Had he foreseen the dislocations of two world wars, the Great Depression, and regional conflicts that would mar the progress of the new age, he might have been less optimistic. But in some ways he was right. For it was in this century that the young Dominion of Canada changed from a dependent colony to a strong and prosperous nation and an important middle power.

The first great catalyst in that maturation was the world war of 1914–18. From a sparse population of less than eight million, Canada raised over 600,000 servicemen and women. Of these some 60,000 able-bodied people — soldiers, sailors, airmen, nursing sisters — would never return. And about 140,000 suffered wounds and disabilities.

But losses aside, the Canadian Expeditionary Force in France and Flanders made contributions to victory all out of proportion to its numbers and the population that raised it. And though our troops fought well at many battles in the war, it was at Vimy Ridge in April 1917 that they captured the world's attention. There, in a carefully planned and brilliantly executed manoeuvre, the Canadian Corps dislodged the tenacious German forces from their commanding position on the Vimy heights. For two and a half years, the enemy had defied all Allied attempts to take the ridge. Then the Canadians, fighting for the first time as a unified and clearly identified body under British commander Lieutenant-General Sir Julian Byng, arrived.

Some of "Byng's boys" put their backs into it, pushing a Canadian Corps truck through the muddy fields at Vimy in April 1917.

German soldiers rush from their dugouts, surrendering to the first advance of Canadian troops on the devastated Vimy heights.

Delegates to a 1919 provincial convention of the Great War Veterans Association, the prime mover for veterans' unity after 1918 and the parent of The Royal Canadian Legion.

Opposite: Field-Marshall Viscount Byng of Vimy as governor general of Canada in 1924. He led Canadian troops to victory at Vimy Ridge and was later named patron of the Canadian Legion at its founding convention in 1925.

Today one of the world's most magnificent war memorials marks the spot where 10,600 Canadians fell casualty. But in a sense this monument also commemorates a birth. For it is often observed that it was on the muddy, blasted fields of Vimy that Canadians clearly established their new national identity and completed the process begun 50 years earlier at Confederation.

But the young nation would undergo many trials, and one of these was to be the repatriation of the hundreds of thousands of returning servicemen. Throughout the war, groups of medically discharged soldiers drifted home. As the conflict wound down,

the numbers swelled, and with them the difficulties. When the conflict finally ended with the capture of the Belgian city of Mons on November 11, 1918, the influx of veterans began in earnest. In less than a year 350,000 returned to Canada from overseas and 73,000 soldiers still in Canada were demobilized. With the 170,000 already discharged during the war and the 25,000 ex-British servicemen in Canada, it was a staggering number to be reabsorbed into the population of eight million. Nor was the task made any easier by the fact that the soldiers and the society they had left to defend had virtually outgrown each other.

Soldiers seasoned by months in the unspeakable conditions of the trenches felt alienated from the new civilian society. Early returnees were met by rampant inflation and a host of new industries that had sprung up to fuel the war effort. Rural people had flocked to the cities, women had entered the industrial workplace and were seeking the vote. Many jobs were filled by recent immigrants from non-English-speaking countries. And many people who had stayed behind had blatantly prospered. The veterans rightly wanted the rewards owed them by the country they had left to protect and that now seemed to be shutting them out.

In the shock and isolation of readjustment, the veterans turned to soldiers' clubs and regimental associations to recapture the camaraderie and sense of purpose they had known in the forces. Gradually the circles outgrew their social aims and began to concentrate on the pressing problems faced by veterans. At first the prime concerns were decent hospitals and proper treatment for the war-wounded, but soon longer-term issues came to the fore: pensions, war allowances, the care of the dependants of the dead and disabled, claims adjustment, and the federal legislation to govern all of this.

In the period after the war, numerous veterans' groups took shape. Some represented those with specific war-related problems: the Tuberculous Veterans Association, the Sir Arthur Pearson Club for Blinded Soldiers and Sailors, the Disabled Veterans Association, the War Amputations Association, the Disabled Veterans of Alberta, the Canadian Pensioners Association. Others took their title from members' military branches: the Naval Veterans Association, the Royal North West Mounted Police Veterans Association. Another category was named for the war in question — the Great War Veterans Association of Canada, the South African Veterans Association — and still another chose more general names related to service: the Grand Army of United Veterans, the Imperial Veterans in Canada, and the Canadian Legion of Ex-Servicemen.

Field-Marshall Earl Haig of Bemersyde, commander-in-chief of the British armies in France and Flanders, 1915–18. An architect of the British Empire Service League, Haig also promoted the unity of Canadian veterans and became grand president of the Canadian Legion, 1925–28.

The pre-eminent group among these was the Great War Veterans Association (GWVA). During its nine-year life from 1917 to 1926, it attracted membership in 700 branches across Canada, and through the voice of its monthly magazine, *The Veteran*, espoused the veterans' cause in political and public circles. Though by no means the only voice to be raised on behalf of ex-servicemen, the collective opinion represented by the GWVA definitely had the ear of government.

First formed in 1917 and formally incorporated in 1921, the association became the major counsellor to government on veterans' affairs. It fostered the formation of the 1923 Royal Commission on Pensions and Re-Establishment and acted as a central agency for settling claims arising from war service, handling 82,000 claims in its first seven years. The government accepted many of the GWVA's recommendations for reabsorption measures and took advice from its leaders on the development of the soldiers' land settlement scheme of 1919. In the light of Legion history, it is interesting to note that though the GWVA made the immediate needs of ex-servicemen and their dependants its priority, it soon developed a broader mandate: working for a better society and building up the young Canadian nation.

And the nation could well use such an attitude. For as the great war machine reversed its engines, the temporary prosperity it had generated collapsed. Canada was once again in an economic depression every bit as grim as that of 1913–15, which the war effort had ended. The popular view of the 1920s is one of economic boom and social progress — mass production, motorcars, telephones, stock-market fortunes, jazz, short skirts, rum runners, women's suffrage, oil in Alberta, fabulous mines in British Columbia and Ontario. But the early years of the decade were actually ones of hardship. By 1921 the post-war slump saw 300,000 Canadians out of work, many of them returned soldiers. To make matters worse, they were competing for jobs with the thousands of immigrants who docked in boatloads every month.

Though the government, through its Department of Soldiers Civil Re-Establishment, was encouraging businesses to rehire returned service people and giving preference to veterans for civil-service posts, unemployment was a major concern. Those who were disabled by service had special problems, and often had trouble establishing military duty as the cause of their infirmity. As well, the government was still inexperienced in operating the machinery governing veterans' affairs. True, a crude system had been established to deal with claims arising from the South African War, in which 7,000 Canadian troops had contributed to the British victory over the Boers, but it was woefully inadequate to deal with the huge numbers of Great War veterans.

It was becoming clear that only a strong and united voice could achieve the kind of government policy and broad social aims veteran leaders advocated. So in addition to pleading the veterans' cause with almost revolutionary fervour, the GWVA also began to advocate the unity of all servicemen's groups. Only in unity could they procure the best treatment and attract the estimated 80 per cent of ex-servicemen who belonged to no veterans' association whatsoever.

Though every issue of *The Veteran* eloquently promoted the cause, it was to be a protracted struggle, for the forces of disunity seemed stronger. Economic and social forces beyond their control were dividing the men who had fought with such cohesion at Vimy and Ypres. Some of the divisions were based on class: haves versus have-nots. There was also great hostility in the West toward the East, the West convinced it had made disproportionate sacrifices of its finest young men while the industrial East had battened off the factories fuelling the war effort. Because of the huge losses of life among the rank and file, there was lingering hostility toward the officers, who had blithely assumed that they would lead the men in peace as they had in war. And it was to the government's advantage to have the veterans split apart. Nothing is harder to manage politically than a large, united interest group.

But gradually the forces of disunity began to wear down, partly through the natural attrition of time, partly through the gradual easing of the depression at mid-decade, and partly through a realistic assessment of the situation. Little would be accomplished at such cross-purposes. The GWVA, through the efforts of its determined and controversial leader, C. Grant MacNeil, became the chief motor behind unification. It had seen the bitterly divisive differences of British veterans overcome in the creation of the British Legion in 1921, and in the same year had promoted the formation in Canada of the Dominion Veterans Alliance, a loose federation of groups pledged to full amalgamation.

The architect of the British Legion and, later the same year, of the British Empire Service League formed at an international conference in Cape Town, South Africa, was the charismatic Earl Haig. As commander-in-chief of the British forces in France and Flanders, he had led the Allies to victory in 1918. Haig desperately aspired to the unification of all veterans in the Empire and was keenly aware that Canada was the only imperial

Lieutenant-General Sir Richard Turner acted as Haig's deputy in Canada to further the amalgamation of all ex-servicemen. As chairman of the Winnipeg conference, he presided over the Legion's formation, and was named both honorary president, 1925, and grand president, 1942–48.

Lieutenant-General Sir Percy Lake, a veteran of the British army in India, Egypt, and the Middle East who had retired to British Columbia, served as first Legion president, 1925–28. His term set the assertive pattern for Legion representations to the government.

dominion lacking a united service organization.

As a constituent member of the British Empire Service League, the GWVA urged Haig and the BESL to visit Canada, and in 1925 the BESL chose Ottawa as the site of its convention. After the congress, Haig made a grand tour of the country, whistle-stopping across the land to the cheers of Canadians everywhere. His visit helped dispel the effects of several years of economic gloom, much as the royal wedding did in Britain in 1981. He pleaded the cause of unity to veterans and public alike, and though some have disputed his motives, most agree on his effect. For if critics argue that Haig's real desire was to strengthen a flagging devotion to the Empire and to secure strong military support for Britain in the event of another war, four organizations came forward in support of unity before he left Canada. These were the GWVA, the Tuberculous Veterans, the Canadian Legion, and the Naval Veterans.

Haig had in Canada a willing trustee of the unity movement, the Quebec general Sir Richard Turner. Turner's rank appealed to the disaffected officers, and his informal connection with the GWVA defused the hostility of other groups to that dominant body. Under the chairmanship of Turner, the GWVA organized a national conference to take place in Winnipeg's stately Marlborough Hotel, November 25 through 28, 1925. As delegates from interested veterans' groups converged on the central Canadian city that had made outstanding contributions to the Canadian Corps and had later elected a veteran as mayor, the stage was set. Two days later most of them would emerge as members of a new cohesive voice, the Canadian Legion of the British Empire Service League.

Despite the hesitancy of groups representing veterans with special disablements to sink their identity in a mainstream organization, most differences were overcome. In fact, the most heated debate revolved around the choice of a name. Loyal to the Crown, the GWVA had earlier proposed the title

of the British Legion in Canada, but it was conference chairman Richard Turner who put forward the name that carried, the Canadian Legion of the British Empire Service League.

Underscoring the prevailing sentiment of unity — ultimately only two major delegate groups, the Army and Navy Veterans and the War Amputations Association, would decline to join the new organization — the conference unanimously elected as president Sir Percy Lake, a retired British general from Victoria, British Columbia, who had seen service in the Middle East, Egypt, and India. Saluting the imperial allegiance of the new organization were the honorary positions conferred on Edward, Prince of Wales, Earl Haig, and Lord Byng, by then the governor general of Canada. Sir Richard Turner and Sir Arthur Currie, a true citizen soldier and native British Columbian who had led the Canadian Corps in the Great War, were also singled out for honorific roles.

The Legion's new constitution established it as a non-sectarian, non-political body with broad objectives. These encompassed loyalty to Canada and the Empire and to the principles of the British constitution; the welfare of all veteran comrades and their dependants; the commemoration and appreciation of the sacrifices of the fallen and the survivors; and social and philanthropic efforts for the good of society as a whole. These aims, and the executive and financial structure of the new institution, derived largely from those of its parent, the GWVA. They have survived with surprisingly little change down to the present.

And so, almost ten years later, the loyal get-together spirit of Vimy reasserted itself to gather veterans into a unified collective force. It would be some months before the new Legion, based in Ottawa, was formally chartered and more before it was able to take over the operative reins of veterans' affairs from the GWVA. But, buoyed by the new economic boom, it was with celebration and optimism that the delegates left Winnipeg, proud of their accomplishment and confident of the new era.

3 *Milestones*

Soaring on the updraft of economic prosperity, the new-fledged Legion entered its first year. Organizationally it had a lot to do. It had to convert its formal unity into fact and establish a financial structure to make itself solvent. At the same time it was assuming the complex adjustment and advocacy work of its parent and trying to attract the thousands of veterans who belonged to no association at all. What's more, the Legion had to weave the lingering identities of its dozen member groups into a new seamless whole.

By the time of its first Dominion Convention in January 1927, the Legion had gone a long way toward realizing these goals — despite being hit amidships by a sudden rumour that it was really a proto-Fascist fifth column bent on the destruction of British democracy!

But internal organization and public relations aside, the Legion had its work cut out in veterans' affairs. With 4,000 new members a month to care for, it soon saw a clear need for better benefits and compensation. And with its quick formation of a committee to propose amendments to federal legislation, Sir Percy Lake's first administration set the assertive pattern that has guided the Legion's relations with Ottawa ever since.

The circumstances of pensioned veterans were, of course, anything but static; and the legislation and procedures providing for their compensation could not remain static either. As the cost of living spiralled upwards with the boom of the Jazz Age, the plight of veterans on fixed compensation became intolerable. Some who had taken up farming under the soldiers' land scheme found themselves with crushing debts, soaring costs in equipment and seed, and the dismal prospect of abandoning their farms. Some veterans, married after their discharge from service, were dying, leaving widows and children unprotected by the usual dependants' compensation. And as the ex-service population grew older, a new disability became obvious: certain veterans were clearly burned out and prematurely aged by the shock of war, and though ineligible for regular pensions, they were every bit as needy as those with injuries from shrapnel, chlorine gas, or tuberculosis. And as usual, there were the delays and arbitrary injustices suffered by those who make application to a large government programme.

Determined to solve these problems, the early Legion presidents — Sir Percy Lake, Major-General Leo LaFlèche, Sir Arthur Currie, Brigadier-General Alex Ross, to name some — set the pace for the forceful efforts of later leaders. Their campaigns have brought Canadian veterans one of the most progressive and comprehensive charters of rights in the world and one that has been widely imitated.

The work of the early presidents continued even after the stock-market crash of 1929 busted the boom and ushered in the Great Depression, with its falling prices, unemployment, soup lines, Prairie droughts, and government cutbacks. Though treading a delicate line between veterans' needs and fiscal constraints, the Legion continued to espouse employment schemes, reduced debt for veteran farmers, better insurance plans, and more realistic pensions. Even in the dark days of 1930 it managed, under the leadership of President LaFlèche to secure a new veterans' allowance and improvements in the Pension Act.

Later, every time some new situation arose, the Legion would respond with the quick reflexes expected of fighting men. Whether it was periodic jumps in the cost of living, the outbreak of World War II and the influx of a new young veteran into the older ex-service population after 1945, the Cold War, or changing social and economic structures at any time — the Legion rose to meet them with strong opinions and constructive proposals.

Nor has it confined its vision to veterans' interests alone, but has focused on a widening range of issues: immigration and national defence; physical fitness and athletic excellence; scholarship and education; medicine; youth and the aged; the integrity of Canadian family and community life; and national unity.

To do justice to the Legion's six decades of struggle and advance would take more space than these pages allow. But here, at a glance, are some of the milestones and high points of those 60 successful years.

The gold-wrought badge of the Canadian Legion of the British Empire Service League, presented in 1926 by Manitoba veterans to Lord Byng. In 1958, when the BESL changed its name to the British Commonwealth Ex-Services League, the Legion shortened its name to the Canadian Legion and in 1960 added the term "Royal." In 1962 the current Legion badge replaced the one shown here.

1925
- The formation of the Canadian Legion of the British Empire Service League, based in Ottawa and a constituent member of the three-million-strong BESL.

1926
- *The Legionary* supersedes the GWVA's *The Veteran* as the new voice of the Canadian Legion.
- The first Legion badge, designed by Winnipeg's George Inglis and worked in gold, is given to Governor General Byng.

- The first Ladies Auxiliaries are organized.
- The official Legion charter is granted by the secretary of state, making unification law.
- The Legion holds its first Poppy Day.

1927
- The first Dominion Convention meets in Winnipeg in January. With Legion membership now numbering 20,000, this "Veterans' Parliament" produces a comprehensive set of proposals to government on veterans' affairs.

The Legion holds its first Dominion Convention in Winnipeg, 1927. Showing the new influence wielded by unified veterans, delegates vote for a review of pension legislation that results in far-reaching amendments.

N LEGION OF THE B·E·S·L·
24TH–29TH, 1927

A 1952 cover of *The Legionary* commemorates the Vimy Pilgrimage of 1936 with a view of the splendid war memorial unveiled at Vimy in the same year.

1930

- The War Veterans Allowance Act is passed, providing compensation for those prematurely aged and incapacitated by their military services.

1931

- The first national Remembrance Day takes place in Ottawa with 50,000 in attendance. Legion representations resulted in an act of Parliament to set aside Armistice Day as an official day of observance.

1936

- The Veterans Assistance (Rattray) Commission is set up to develop jobs for unemployed veterans. One scheme results in the formation of the Corps of Commissionaires in 1937.
- The Vimy Pilgrimage transports 6,400 men, women, and children to the site of the famous victory, a tremendous undertaking given the bleak economic times. King Edward VIII, soon to abdicate, unveils a magnificent memorial crowning 250 acres of French land donated to Canada.

1938

- A permanent Legion education committee is established.
- The Legion formulates a plan for all-out war against nazism.

1939

- The National Veterans Survey uncovers 100,000 World War I veterans ready to serve in wartime, from whose ranks the Veterans Guard of Canada is formed.
- Canada's National War Memorial is unveiled in Ottawa by the new king, George VI, during a May royal tour.

1939–1945

- Canadian Legion War Services and Educational Services ensure that World War II service people fare better than their predecessors in World War I. The Legion provides funds, canteens, service clubs, luxury items, entertainment, and, most important, continuing education for Canada's armed forces at home and overseas. It also helps form the Veterans Guard of Canada.

1943–1945

- The Veterans Charter, a comprehensive body of legislation easing the reinstatement of returned service people, grows out of the Legion's concern that the young World War II veterans be spared the disadvantages suffered by their World War I predecessors.

Badly wounded at Mont Sorrel in 1916, Major-General Leo R. LaFlèche of Ottawa survived to become first Legion treasurer in 1925 and president, 1929–31.

Major John S. Roper of Halifax, president, 1931–34, steered the Legion through delicate negotiations with the federal government in the early years of the Depression.

Benefits include land settlement, cash gratuities, good medical treatment, compensation, and university or vocational training.

1944
- The Department of Veterans Affairs comes into being, after the Legion convinces Ottawa that veterans' interests would be better served by one special department.

1949
- Newfoundland becomes Canada's tenth province, and its chapter of the GWVA joins the Legion. Membership approaches 100,000.
- Operation Vote, a successful Legion media campaign, urges Canadians to exercise their democratic franchise in the federal elections.

1951–52
- The Watts cost-of-living campaign responds to rocketing prices after the outbreak of the Korean War. Eventually veterans win a one-third increase in pensions, the dropping of a proposed government means test, and some increases in veterans' allowances.

1955
- Dominion President the Very Reverend John O. Anderson issues a challenge to the Legion to refocus its sights away from veterans' affairs and toward general community service.

1956
- The Legion shows its serious interest in Canadian sports by pledging financial support for Olympic-calibre track and field training for young athletes.

1958
- The Canadian Legion of the British Empire Service League shortens its name to the Canadian Legion. Members number 220,000.
- Legion House, a modern, million-dollar building, becomes the new headquarters of the Legion's Dominion Command.

1960
- The Queen assents to the addition of ''Royal'' to the Canadian Legion's name.

Brigadier-General Alex Ross of Yorkton, Saskatchewan, president, 1934–38, presided over the great undertaking that was the Vimy Pilgrimage of 1936.

The Very Reverend John O. Anderson, Anglican Dean of Ottawa, served as president, 1954–56, and led the Legion's move away from specialization in veterans' affairs and into widespread community service.

1962
- A new Legion badge appears, designed by Lieutenant-Commander Alan Beddoe, OBE.
- The dynamic National Working Committee on Membership is formed, and is followed by other important national internal programmes on such issues as leadership and organization.

1962–1972
- The Legion organizes pilgrimages to the gravesites of Canadian service people buried in Holland. Some 2,000 family members are involved in these trips. The visits result in The Royal Canadian Legion's becoming godfather to Holland's Prince Florin.

1963–1969
- The Royal Canadian Legion Sports Training Plan begins to train coaches to develop top Canadian athletes. Former British national coach Geoffrey Dyson heads the programme, which publishes *The Coaching Review* and the *Track and Field Annual Review*.

1966
- As a member of the British Commonwealth Ex-Services League, the Legion accepts responsibility for veterans' welfare in the Caribbean.

1968
- The Woods Committee, appointed as a result of Legion efforts, leads to a restructured Pension Act in the early 1970s, which increases benefits for disability pensioners and their dependants.

1969
- *Legion* magazine, a modern, trade-style periodical, replaces the worthy *Legionary*.

1970
- Looking ahead, the Legion broadens its ranks by admitting, as social members, non-military fraternal affiliates.

1972
- The Legion prepares for the future by opening its doors to associate members, the sons and daughters of Legion members and eligibles. RCMP veterans are admitted.

1973
- The recommendations of a Joint Study Group including Legion representatives bring increases in the basic pension rates plus annual increments in accordance with rises in the cost of living—the culmination of a decades-long battle for realistic pensions and allowances.

1974
- ACTION (A Commitment To Improve Our Nation), a broadly focused social action programme, seeks to strengthen the quality of Canadian life by countering drug abuse, the decline of the family, the deterioration of the environment, and failings in the legal and justice systems.

1975
- In the year of its Golden Anniversary, the Legion donates a spectacular illumination system for the National War Memorial.
- The Legion donates $50,000 to the Canada Studies Foundation to help publish a study on Canadian government.

1976
- The Legion joins the World Veterans Federation.

1977–1978
- The Legion forms a task force to inform Canadians about the crisis in national unity. A brief to the federal government has tremendous impact, and its recommendations are adopted in most respects.

1980
- Full voting rights are granted to associate members, assuring them of a say in the Legion's future.

1981
- The Aging Veterans Program guarantees the elderly a dignified living in their own homes with medical, domestic, and groundskeeping help through financial assistance from Veterans Affairs.

The Canadian military cemetery at Bergen op Zoom, Holland. From 1965 to 1975 the Legion organized visits to such gravesites for the families of Canadians buried there.

The endless campaign for better pensions is typified by this 1957 illustration from *The Legionary*. It shows how the gap between pensioners' annual incomes and those of current servicemen and unskilled labourers had steadily widened since the 1920s, when they were roughly par.

1982
- The spouses of Legion members are admitted as associates with full voting rights.

1985
- In its Diamond Jubilee year, the Legion's membership approaches 600,000.

4 *World War II*

When the shadow of war darkened the face of Europe in September 1939, the Legion was already prepared. It had soon recognized the rebirth of an old enemy, German militarism, and unlike many of its complacent countrymen, was not taken unawares by the outbreak of hostilities. And throughout the war years, the Legion would wage its own battles on three main fronts: urging the government to a more concentrated war effort; providing educational and humane services for the welfare of Canadian troops; and helping the government develop an effective rehabilitation plan for the new generation of veterans.

The Legion and Canada's War Effort
Sensing the advent of war after the Munich Affair of 1938, the Legion immediately put all its facilities at the disposal of Prime Minister

Many a homesick young serviceman's overseas stay was made more cheerful by the friendly staff and affordable comforts at Legion clubs like this one in London.
Opposite: Looking ahead to postwar rehabilitation, the Legion sponsored many educational courses. Here service women and men attend a machine shop class in British Columbia.

These Legion women stand ready to welcome troops returning home to Quebec City.

Mackenzie King. It stressed the need for national preparedness and criticized both the trusting smugness of the Canadian public and the country's inadequate home defences.

The next year, the Legion and other ex-service groups undertook a national survey of veterans, which registered over 100,000 experienced men willing to serve in any way they could. The Legion wanted protection for vital installations against possible sabotage,

Canadian servicemen, with CLWS supervisors in the background, look up from their letters home in a London writing room.

Shooting a little pool in the recreation room of the #10 General Hospital in England.

and to this end helped form the Veterans Home Guard in 1940. Backed by reserve corps and eventually becoming an official unit of the Canadian Army, the Veterans Guard of Canada, as it later became known, drew on thousands of Great War personnel to guard power plants, bridges, waterways, factories, communications installations and prisoner-of-war camps.

As the war dragged on, making it clear there would be no quick and easy victory against the Nazi aggressors, the Legion spoke out against the cautious and lacklustre war effort of the King government. Calling for a total mobilization of human, industrial, agricultural, and mineral resources for the forceful prosecution of the war, it gained wide support from citizens' groups and the press. It supported the

maintenance of maximum armed services; and after the heavy casualties of the ill-fated Dieppe Raid in 1942, began to urge the government to conscript soldiers to shore up the badly depleted troops overseas.

As in the Great War, the conscription issue became a divisive force in Canadian life. It was only after a cautious referendum released him from a pre-election vow not to institute conscription that King eventually began to draft soldiers for home defence only. Ultimately, though, some 16,000 drafted servicemen fought overseas for Canada. Throughout the furore, the Legion steadfastly contended that compulsory selective service was the only fair and democratic way to solve the manpower crisis on the firing line and lend the gallant volunteers at the front the support they

Distributing cigarettes to servicemen. Legion mobile canteens were kept busy supplying hot drinks, chocolate, writing paper, and other amenities to the armed forces at home and abroad.

deserved. Its unwavering support of this very unpopular measure strengthened its public profile and brought many new veterans into its ranks after the war.

Canadian Legion War Services

If the Great War veterans of the Legion knew how formidable an enemy the young servicemen of the new conflict faced, they were also well aware of other foes. Among these were deprivation, the edgy boredom of awaiting combat, a sense of being abandoned by their country, disruption of their education, and, perhaps worst of all, worry over their unprotected families at home.

No one knew better than the Great War veterans how these psychological cancers could eat away at the effectiveness of troops in the field and ultimately create a bitterness that could impoverish a whole generation. And so, in 1939, the Legion set up its Canadian Legion War Services Inc., a non-profit organization working under the Auxiliary Services of the Department of National Defence. The CLWS was to provide a broad range of vital support systems to the services: continuing education, personal counselling and chaplains, entertainment, travel opportunities, recreation and sports, luxury items, leave hostels and reading rooms, mobile canteens, and liaison services.

Overseas and at home, CLWS mobile canteens were on hand with hot drinks, chocolate, cigarettes, and free writing paper. The operation established affordable hostels and service clubs for soldiers on leave, and comfortable reading rooms where they could catch up on the news from home. Legion personnel would pile into assault boats right alongside the troops and go ashore with them to the war arena. CWLS stage shows and movies delighted troops in Canada, Europe, and England, and enlisted men breathed a little easier knowing that the Legion was working with social agencies to ease the financial hardship of their families at home. At war's end the organization was able to hand over more than one million dollars to the Benevolent Fund for the welfare of veterans and their dependants.

Educational Services

But important as these homestyle comforts and general amenities were for the Canadian forces' morale, it was the CLWS's educational services that probably made the most lasting impact. In effect, this programme cosmopolitanized a whole generation of servicemen, boosted Canadian literacy, fostered the standardization of educational qualifications from province to province, and contributed greatly to Canada's post-war revitalization in business and the professions.

With the founding of a permanent education council under Lieutenant-Colonel Wilfrid Bovey in 1938, the Legion acknowledged two things. First, the disruption of a young person's normal education through military service could prove a handicap every bit as disabling as a war injury. And second, the modern, highly mechanized war that seemed just around the corner would require servicemen to be better educated and better equipped to make individual decisions. The educational division of the CLWS assisted members of the armed forces in Canada, overseas, and even in prisoner-of-war camps to use inactive time during the war to study. Later these courses were phased into ongoing, post-discharge programmes for veterans.

To this end, the CLWS worked with provincial departments of education and Canadian and European universities to provide thousands of courses, ranging from elementary-school subjects and high-school and vocational training to university undergraduate and postgraduate studies. It published over two million standardized textbooks to make

Montreal's Britannia Branch puts on a wartime dinner for dozens of service personnel.

It's snow on the palm trees for Christmas 1943 at the Gower Street Club in London.

the quality of the courses uniform and acceptable to different provincial authorities. In fact, the Legion's little gold and blue texts became a staple item in the kitbags of thousands of soldiers. When the mortars fell silent in the bombed-out cities of the war theatre, you could often hear the clack of student typewriters, the nasals and gutturals of high-school French and German, and the logical exposition of geometry theorems.

During its life, the Legion's Khaki College taught over 200,000 service students in over 11,000 classes that ranged from the three R's to advanced academic subjects, bookkeeping, agriculture, and skilled trades. One young officer training in England continued his engineering studies, and before his regiment landed in Normandy, had earned his Ph.D. from Cambridge University. And having got their start in the CLWS wartime education programme, thousands more continued their studies after discharge and became highly trained professionals, businessmen, and skilled tradesmen, working at a level they might never have achieved on their own.

Rehabilitation

While thoroughly embroiled in such wartime concerns, the Legion was characteristically thinking ahead to post-discharge rehabilitation. With the bitter postwar battles of the earlier great conflict behind it, the Legion knew that the soldiers, sailors, and aviators who had won the war often had to fight equally hard to win the peace. As early as 1940, Legion leaders began presenting Ottawa with detailed briefs on the re-establishment of the new veterans, and pressing for humane measures that would somehow compensate for the bitter disappointments dealt their own generation of servicemen. Their blueprint for total rehabilitation was published in a booklet and distributed by the thousands overseas. It undoubtedly attracted many of the new war veterans into the Legion.

To make a long and complex story short, the Legion's tireless efforts on the veterans' behalf eventually resulted in a legislative package known as the Veterans Charter. Early in the war, the government agreed to grant the new group of veterans the same entitlements in medical treatment, pensions, and allowances as Great War ex-servicemen enjoyed, adding a new scale of vocational training and living allowances. Later, new acts enlarged the apparatus set up to ensure the smooth and satisfactory reintegration of demobilized per-

Against the ornate decor of the Canadian Legion Club in Paris, acrobats perform at a floor show in 1945. All during the war, Legion-sponsored concerts, movies, and shows lifted the spirits of service people both in Canada and overseas.

The Legionettes of the Canadian Legion All Stars pose in top form in Montreal.
Below: Suggesting warmer climes and easier times, entertainers in a Latin-style show form a conga line for the camera in wartime London.

sonnel into civilian life. The Civil Reinstatement Act, for example, assured veterans of being rehired by former employers for whom they had worked at least three months before enlistment. The Post-Discharge Re-Establishment Order provided unemployment benefits and education. Veterans could now pick up their education where the CLWS had left off, and thousands continued with business, academic, and vocational training.

A more workable land settlement scheme, the Veterans Land Act, established service people in farming and commercial fishing in areas of stable markets and high yields. The 1944 Gratuities Act provided cash grants and financial credits to returnees to help them get a head start in civilian life. In the same year, the government yielded to suggestions put forward earlier by the Legion's vigorous wartime president, Alex Walker, and set up the

Department of Veterans Affairs to replace the several departments and agencies that had shared responsibility for ex-service people. By the end of the war, Canadian veterans were blessed with an enviable body of protective legislation that would be imitated in other Commonwealth countries.

As proof of its success, the huge numbers of returned army, navy, and airforce personnel were reabsorbed with relative ease into the booming postwar economy. Though most returned to their former jobs, 50,000 went on to university, 130,000 took other vocational training, and 22,000 took up farming. Over 250,000 used their re-establishment credits as a leg up in the new postwar society. The Legion had played a large part in preventing a repetition of the chaos and dislocation that had followed demobilization in 1918.

Though the machinery was now satisfactorily in place, the Legion continued its vigilance, constantly evaluating the adequacy of the law and the effectiveness of its application. Acting as liaison between Ottawa and individual applicants, it processed thousands of claims for benefits through its Dominion and provincial service bureaus. And it saw that, after 1951, Korean War veterans enjoyed all the privileges accorded their predecessors.

But with most of the legislative territory conquered, it was time for the Legion to turn its gaze outward, to Canadian society at large. In a landmark address of 1955, Dominion President the Very Reverend John O. Anderson challenged Legionnaires to redirect their efforts to full-scale community service. The challenge was heartily accepted, and that takes us out of the past and right into the contemporary life of The Royal Canadian Legion today.

Sergeant Alex Walker of Calgary, the first Legion president not of officer rank. He led the vigorous campaign for an all-out war effort and enlightened rehabilitation measures for World War II veterans during his wartime term, 1940–46.

PART TWO
LOOKING AHEAD

5 Legion Mosaic

The preceding pages present the history of The Royal Canadian Legion as a mirror of Canada's history in the 20th century. Far from growing in isolation, the organization has developed in response to most of the major international events and national upheavals of the past 70 years. And, in a similar way, the 600,000 people of today's Legion reflect the complex cultural mosaic of Canada.

Canada emerged from status as a British colony and grew into an open society comprising many ethnic groups, and with her the Legion has expanded from its beginnings as a British-Canadian and masculine organization led by aristocrats to an egalitarian body that cuts across age, sex, nationality, mother tongue, and class. In 1,800 branches, scattered the length and breadth of Canada's four million square miles, Legion people are drawn from many religious and political persuasions, income and educational levels, occupations, and lifestyles. They may be 95 or 25, grandmothers or students, Ph.D.s or public-school graduates. They are fishermen and farmers, business people and lawyers, civil servants, Supreme Court justices, and clergymen.

Though they hail from diverse ethnic backgrounds—from Inuit and Indian to Greek, Jewish, Ukrainian, Polish, and French Canadian—all Legion members are united by common ideals. They are joined by a spirit of volunteerism and a dedication to peace and democracy, patriotism and commemoration, mutual help, and wide community service.

Membership in the Legion has recently been possible on increasingly broad grounds. The largest category of member—about half the membership—is made up of men and women who saw service in World War II. About one-quarter are voting associates, the spouses, sons, and daughters of members, or those eligible for membership. Half as many again are ex-service personnel from various corps, and much smaller numbers are represented by veterans of World War I, current service personnel, and veterans of the Korean War. A few members are veterans of the RCMP. Some of the most dynamic Legion people are the 90,000 members of the Ladies Auxiliaries of various branches and commands. And the Legion also makes room for honorary members and fraternal affiliates—people who support its objectives without qualifying for membership on the usual grounds.

With its large and diverse following, the Legion has become both a strong national body based in the capital, and a grass-roots community movement reaching into the tiniest rural hamlets. It has spoken to the government and public with a voice as strong as the largest citizens' groups and labour organizations. At the same time, it has rivalled the service of the largest organized charities and social agencies—in everything, that is, but the publicity received, for the Legion prefers to function in a low-key, unassuming manner.

Despite their military aura, Legion branches are places where members associate and co-operate freely, leaving social status, politics, and religion behind. The units operate quite autonomously under charter from Dominion Command in Ottawa. Branches are organized

Standing tall at 90, Jack Collier of Hamilton is still active in his colour party.

Overleaf: A Legion parade stands out against the sombre backdrop of the hills around the Okanagan Valley in Lumby, British Columbia.

into zones and districts that fall under the jurisdiction of provincial commands. These report back to Dominion Command, which supervises the Legion on the national level, makes representations to the federal government, and operates the national Service Bureau.

The financial structure of the Legion is supported by modest annual branch dues and per capita taxes levied by Dominion and provincial commands. It is non-profit and self-supporting. While commands have a few salaried employees, the main work of the Legion is carried out by its army of volunteers. Through careful investment and the steady acquisition of office buildings, non-profit housing, and branch halls, the organization has evolved into a wealthy one, commanding millions of dollars in fixed and liquid assets and donating millions of dollars a year to philanthropic causes.

Clearly, it is a difficult matter to administer and communicate with such widespread units, and that's where the Legion's Dominion and provincial conventions come in. Provincial meetings are called annually or biennially, and a Dominion Convention is called biennially and held in different regions of the country. At provincial conventions, branch delegates elect officers to the Dominion Executive Council, which governs the Legion between national conventions. Dominion Convention, the final authority of the Legion, determines by majority vote of branch representatives the policy of the Legion on all major subjects. It also elects officers to the Sub-executive Council, which administers the day-to-day operations of the Legion. A system of standing committees addresses specific issues, from pensions and housing to sports.

Headquarters of Dominion Command are located in a six-storey building on Kent Street in downtown Ottawa. Here the national Service Bureau operates, acting as liaison with government departments and commissions and making claims on behalf of thousands of veterans and their dependants, whether Legion members or not. Legion House, as it is

Opposite, top: A line of delegates at the 1984 Dominion Convention in Winnipeg.
Opposite, bottom: Flags steal a march on a parade in Windsor, Ontario.
Top right: Getting in formation for the veterans' parade at the Winnipeg convention.
Bottom right: Each year Legionnaires from Lumby exchange a historic friendship gavel with members of the American Legion from Oroville, Washington.

The Legion is alive and well in almost 2,000 Canadian communities, from large urban centres to remote villages. *Top left:* A snow-capped peak broods over a branch hall in Banff. *Bottom left:* The RCL crest stands out on a downtown Edmonton branch against a surround of modern skyscrapers. *Top right:* Winnipeg's stately Marlborough Hotel, where the Legion began its life in 1925. *Bottom right:* The RCL is very much a part of far-northern centres like Inuvik, where this round church is a striking landmark.

Bright subarctic fireweed flaunts its brief summer glory against a Legion-supported cultural centre in Yellowknife.

known, is also home to *Legion* magazine, a lively periodical published monthly by Canvet Publications Ltd. and issued automatically to all members. The direct descendant of the GWVA's *The Veteran* and of its successor, *The Legionary*, the magazine is an important communications link in the vast Legion network.

And that network is made even larger by The Royal Canadian Legion's membership in two international veterans' organizations: the British Commonwealth Ex-Services League, based in London and the child of Earl Haig's old BESL; and the World Veterans Federation, currently headquartered in Paris. Through its participation in these, the Legion involves itself in the cause of veterans in countries

The RCL's 600,000 members represent many different races, creeds, and walks of life. This Legionnaire is a full-blooded Oneida Indian.

As a young sailor, Jack Smith of the Esquimalt, British Columbia, Legion posed for the famous portrait on the Player's Cigarettes package.

Born in Sweden and a Canadian for many years, this Inuvik charter member has lived all his life north of the Arctic Circle.

where they don't enjoy the hard-won rights Canadian ex-service people do. Canada's special responsibility is the Caribbean, and the Legion lends financial and material support to veterans' organizations throughout the West Indies. Its 70 posts in the United States lend a helping hand to Canadian and British veterans there.

Though clearly absorbed in today's pressing issues, the Legion is also looking ahead. It is looking ahead to the time when it must transfer its legacy to a younger group that, unlike the Legion's founders and present core, has little acquaintance with the rigours of military duty and, fortunately, no experience of war. Anticipating the future, has in fact, always been an overriding Legion concern.

Soon after its formation in 1925, Sir Arthur Currie urged uncommitted veterans to close ranks and ensure the safe transfer of the covenant before it was too late: "The artillery of time," as he eloquently put it, "with its ruthless fire, is against us and yearly leaves its gaps."

In the same spirit, today's Legion is seeking to compensate for the inevitable attrition of time by opening its doors to new, young, non-veteran members. Unlike the early founders, these new ranks may not be citizen soldiers. But they *will* be soldier citizens, who will carry forward the Legion standards to its next century and beyond. And it will be an act of faith and discipline by which both they and Canadian society will profit.

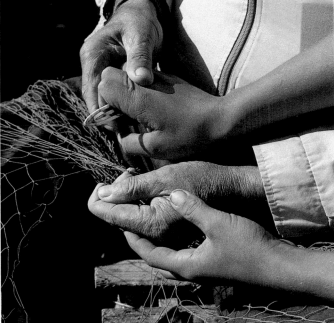

Some Legionnaires are Newfoundland fishermen operating small boats like those moored in the cove above in Quidi Vidi.
Right: Cleaning the catch, mending nets, and drying cod in east-coast fishing centres.

The Legion counts many fine craftsmen and artists among its membership. This veteran constructs accurate models of steam and sailing ships in Nova Scotia.

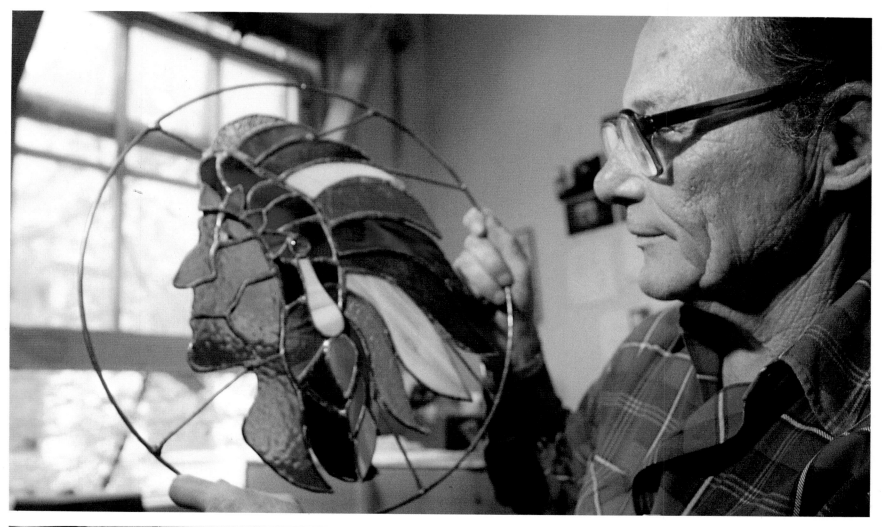

Opposite, top: An amputee who builds wooden miniatures of windmills and other structures.
Opposite, bottom: A Legionnaire painter-farmer-musician.
Above: Working in ornamental stained glass.
Left: Hand-tooled leather wallets are the specialty of this Legionnaire.

Overleaf top: A setting in the elegant gourmet restaurant of the Red Deer, Alberta, Branch.
Middle: Some Legion members, like Sergeant Doug Fletcher, are currently serving in the Canadian Armed Forces.
Bottom: A young member of the Ladies Auxiliary serves up a couple of Prince Edward Island's upper-crustaceans, Legion-style.

The impressive floor geometry of a full session of
Dominion Convention, Winnipeg, 1984.

Above: A service officer counsels a veteran in New Brunswick.
Left: The memorial stained-glass panel at the entrance to a downtown Regina branch.

Opposite, top: A 95-year-old veteran of the World War I nursing corps chats with Legion women in a Sydney, Nova Scotia, veterans' residence.
Opposite, bottom: A veteran member adjusts the beret of a young woman at the Winnipeg convention.

6 Keeping Faith

We will remember them. This promise, in its Latin form of *Memoriam eorum retinebimus*, is the official motto of The Royal Canadian Legion, and one of its most fundamental articles of faith. By it, the Legion commits itself to preserving the memory and honouring the sacrifice of the more than 114,000 Canadians who were killed in conflicts in which Canada participated. The same motto pledges the Legion to keep faith with the ideals for which this great sacrifice was made: world peace, personal freedom, and democratic government.

While it generally prefers to accomplish its work in a quiet, unobtrusive way, the Legion has always cultivated a strong public profile in the solemn celebration of Remembrance Day. This moving ceremony, which each November 11 unites Canadians of all ages across the country, is an event of prime importance in the Legion's calendar. From its earliest years the organization has fostered its observance. In fact, it was largely its representations to Ottawa that brought about an act of Parliament in 1931 that set aside November 11 as a special day of remembrance.

Since that time, the Legion has strongly resisted any attempts to erode the significance

Previous pages: All across Canada, the Legion fosters tributes to those who fall in the service of their country. *Left:* ''Last Post'' at a ceremony in Ontario. *Right:* A monument to northern bush pilots, many of whom were ex-airforce personnel and Legionnaires.

Top: Placing a wreath at a memorial in Yellowknife and playing ''Last Post'' in Truro, Nova Scotia.
Bottom: The grandeur of the National War Memorial in Ottawa and the simple poignancy of a small cenotaph in Woodlands, Manitoba.

Queen Elizabeth and Prince Philip lay a commemorative wreath at a Toronto memorial during the 1984 royal tour.

This monument in Dieppe, New Brunswick, includes stones gathered by schoolchildren from the beaches of the town's namesake in France.

and dignity of Remembrance Day. It has promoted its observance by supporting it as a statutory holiday or urging that it be marked by ceremonies in schools, office complexes, and municipal centres. In the same spirit it has supported the raising of memorial plaques and cenotaphs to Canada's war dead and has called for their upkeep and periodic updating. In 1975, the year of its Golden Anniversary, it

A commemorative garden of scarlet poppies grows outside a branch in Banff.

donated a splendid illumination system to Canada's National War Memorial in Ottawa's Confederation Square, where each November 11 the Legion co-ordinates our national service of commemoration. It has also consistently opposed any attempt to alter the historic Books of Remembrance housed on Parliament Hill, which record the names of our war dead on beautifully illuminated and calligraphed pages.

Similarly, the Legion has spoken out against the use of war memorials around the country as rallying points for recent protest groups that show little appreciation of the sacrifice of those the memorials honour. And it has countered the misinterpretation of such monuments and of Remembrance Day as a celebration of war, for there are no stronger advocates of peace than those who have had direct experience with the devastation of armed conflicts. The greying veterans who gather each year on November 11 saw comrades die, and in many cases suffered grievous injuries themselves. Each Remembrance Day they are rededicating themselves to the preservation of peace, not to the glorification of war.

Closely associated with Remembrance Day is the Poppy campaign, an annual appeal for funds held by individual Legion branches in thousands of Canadian communities in the period before November 11. The scarlet flowers so familiar from Lieutenant-Colonel John McCrae's stirring poem, ''In Flanders Fields,'' became an international symbol of remembrance when a Frenchwoman, Madame Guérin, borrowed the idea in 1918 from a young New York canteen worker to use as a focus for fund-raising in war-torn France. The Flanders poppy was adopted by the British Empire Service League; in Canada, the Legion's parent, the Great War Veterans Association, held its first Poppy Day appeal for funds for needy veterans in November 1921. Each year since then veterans and their colleagues—especially the Ladies Auxiliaries —have sold the simple flowers to raise money for less fortunate comrades. In 1983 almost

Ranks of international representatives stand ready to lay wreaths at the National War Memorial.

The Legion section of a quiet cemetery in Stonewall, Manitoba.

Surmounted by a caribou, this St. John's memorial honours Newfoundlanders who fell in World War I and has an exact counterpart in Beaumont Hamel, Belgium, not far from Vimy Ridge.

Top left: A commemorative cross in Newfoundland, the most easterly memorial in Canada.
Above: A veteran Legionnaire introduces two young sea cadets to books of remembrance in Charlottetown.
Right: Cenotaph and plaque on the grounds of Legion Village, a residential complex in Toronto.

A remembrance service at Winnipeg's war memorial.

Decoration Day in Hamilton.

12 million poppies were distributed.

The poppy has come to mean three things: a visible symbol of remembrance and thanks; a way of raising emergency funds for veterans in difficulty; and a means of providing employment for the disabled ex-service people who produce lapel flowers, wreaths, and crosses through workshops sponsored by the Department of Veterans Affairs. Poppy campaigns are run by individual Legion branches with volunteer labour. Donations from the public are distributed by the branches in accordance with the rules established by Dominion Command. Each year many veterans and their dependants are spared the embarrassment of seeking municipal welfare assistance by appealing to branch poppy funds. This is a gift freely given in memory of fallen comrades to those who are now living in need.

Shortly after the community poppy campaigns comes Remembrance Day. On November 11, the day Canadian troops recaptured the Belgian city of Mons in 1918 and helped end the Great War, people gather at 11 A.M. All across the land, whether in pale autumn sunshine or the first snow flurries of the year, heads bow for a moment's silence. Some hear the mournful strains of the "Last Post," others watch the laying of wreaths, the honouring of the mothers of slain sons and daughters. There are speeches, prayers, and appeals for peace. There are salutes, colour, pageantry; the momentary joining of young and old. But most of all, there is acknowledgement of the enormous contribution to today's society made by the young Canadian soldiers who died many years ago. And among the Legion members present, there is also a determination to maintain the principles they willingly defended.

Top: A commemorative
sculpture in a downtown
Edmonton branch.
Bottom: Canada's oldest
military cemetery, Victoria,
British Columbia.

"We will remember them,"
Vetville, Châteauguay,
Quebec.

7 Branch Life

As we saw, the Legion took its origins from social groups in which returned soldiers could seek comfort in the comradeship and mutual help of fellow veterans. And the fostering of human companionship and co-operation is still one of the Legion's primary goals. Now, of course, the organization has grown to encompass a much broader membership than war veterans, and must continue this expansion if it is to survive. And though it is still dedicated to the needs of ex-servicemen and women, it has long since turned its helping hand to the community at large.

The Legion's few early founders could not have foreseen that it would one day be the country's largest service club — penetrating into almost 2,000 communities and donating an estimated $30 million a year for their benefit, not counting the thousands of hours of voluntary labour on which no figure can be placed. But in centres large and small, urban and rural, Legion branch halls are the focus of a well-rooted social force that combines companionship with philanthropy, social activities with social activism.

Here members of every age and stripe get together for good talk, affordable food and drink, a game of darts, cards, or pool. In friendly Legion clubrooms elderly veterans exchange reminiscences. The recollections are usually funny ones — rarely do they talk about the bad parts — tales of World War I patrols trying to catch a skinny stray pig to roast for Christmas dinner; of World War II soldiers about to sample a donated keg of French apple brandy, only to have it flambéd by an errant German shell falling through the roof. Here Legion members form competitive dart teams, ball clubs, billiards and curling teams, bridge and euchre clubs, pipe bands, and brass bands.

In fact, branch halls are perhaps the closest thing to genuine British public houses that Canadian communities are likely to see. But unlike ordinary pubs or clubrooms, Legion halls are the nerve centres of vigorous social-action programmes that touch many aspects of life around them. With its *laissez faire* policy of "branches know best," the Legion encourages its members to reach out into their local communities wherever there is need. All across the land, hospitals and medical clinics benefit from Legion volunteers and funds donated for vital but costly equipment. In hundreds of communities, rinks, athletic centres, and parks are completed a little faster or substantially improved by Legion cheques. Many a school or home for handicapped children has been the beneficiary of Legion generosity. Other charitable organizations such as the Canadian Red Cross Society and the St. John Ambulance have been the recipients of vans, stretchers, and equipment.

In small communities, the Legion actually assumes the functions handled in larger centres by several other service organizations. It holds blood donor clinics, establishes eye banks and big-brother programmes, provides emergency housing, forms drop-in centres, daycare units, and kindergartens. It runs movie theatres, caters weddings, and offers relief to disaster victims. Many a student's way

The inviting interior of an RCL hall in Newfoundland.

Previous page: Some 250 miles above the Arctic Circle, this log cabin is home to Branch 220, Inuvik, the most northerly Legion hall in Canada.

Yellowknife members raise funds for charity with a gambling casino featuring blackjack and roulette.

Overleaf: A game of blind cribbage in Lynden, Ontario.

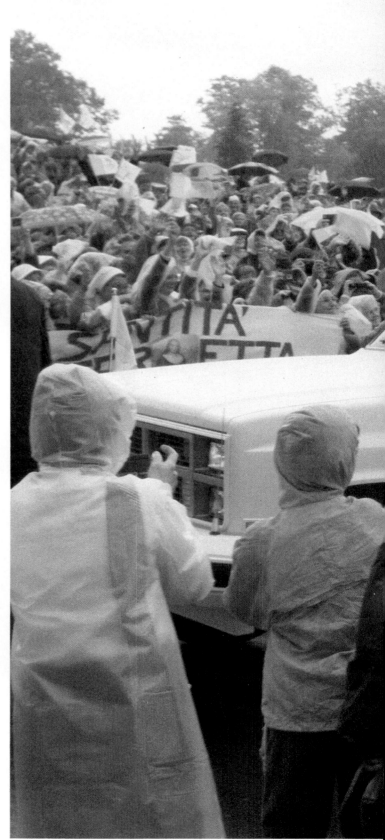

Above, top: Members prepare a striking float featuring
the wild rose of Alberta for a parade in Leduc.
Above, bottom: A bright Legion ''cooler'' covers the
winner of an RCL harness race in Prince Edward Island.

Right: Legionnaires called up for crowd-control duty
during Pope John Paul's visit to Midland, Ontario, 1984.

Above: The fruits of the Nova Scotia summer go into the catering of a regimental reunion in a Truro branch.
Top right: Suitably costumed, senior ladies enjoy a quilting bee in the Hudson, Quebec, Branch.
Bottom right: A ceramics workshop at a drop-in centre in a Vancouver branch.

is made easier by Legion bursaries; many a young athlete's career is given a boost by Legion sports training. And the organization is perhaps the country's largest sponsor of Scouts, Guides, and Cadets.

The elderly, the young, the in-between, all are the targets of Legion programmes. And the dual goal of having fun and raising funds adds up to an inventive, picturesque, and incredibly varied mix of events. Branches in the remotest corner of Canada stage lively and stylish galas appropriate to the region and season. There are salmon derbies in British Columbia; charitable lotteries in Alberta; husky dog sled championships in the North; tuna tournaments in Prince Edward Island. There are Ontario maple sugar festivals; British Columbia bath-tub races, Atlantic harness derbies, Maritime lobster bakes, Prairie corn roasts. There are card parties, dances, parades, spring fishing contests, and winter bonspiels.

The Legion's innovative fund-raising is testimony to the ingenuity of its members. And its community service is witness to the generosity of the Legion spirit. For wherever it sees a need, it quickly responds with the initiative and drive characteristic of its earliest founders — the volunteering spirit of those citizen soldiers who did not wait to be asked.

In period dress, seniors perform a folk dance in the Hudson Legion hall.

To be a vet is to love telling tales and venting opinions. Many branches have a Table of Knowledge just for that purpose, like this one in Brantford, Ontario— appropriately presided over by a large bull.

In Yellowknife the RCL assists a marine rescue program.

Many of the funds raised go toward medical equipment for Canadian hospitals. This laser apparatus used in optical examinations and operations was donated by a an RCL Jewish branch to a Vancouver hospital.

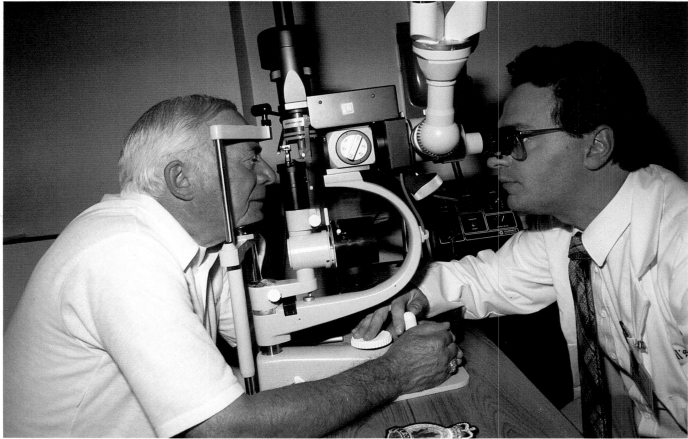

Two members peruse the building plans for a senior
citizens' housing project in Saskatchewan.

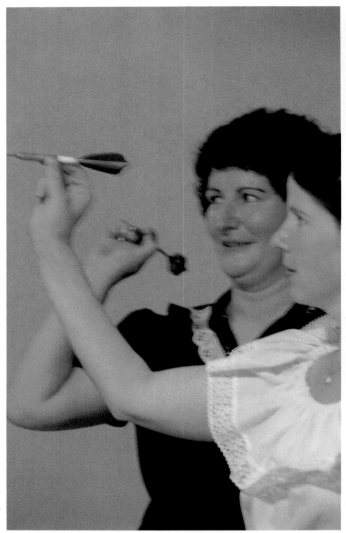
Ladies' darts in a New Brunswick branch.

A Toronto member lines up a great shot in his local hall.

A cribbage player displays his third-in-a-lifetime perfect hand.

A World War I veteran
throws the opening horse-
shoe in a Burk's Falls,
Ontario, match.

Working in a little summer practice for the winter dog sled championships
in the Far North.

Opposite: A member adjusts the shovel hanging ready for action above the Table of Knowledge in the Callander, Ontario, hall.

The interior of an ingenious house built entirely of glass bottles by a Prince Edward Island Legionnaire.

Members pose in front of the half-timbered exterior of the Campbell River Branch in British Columbia.

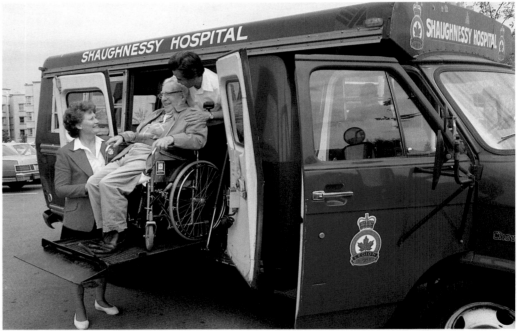

Legion transportation for the disabled in Vancouver.

This handsome brick building is the Valour Road Branch located on a tree-lined street in Winnipeg.

Socializing in the lounge of a Montreal branch.

An RCL hall with a view: Ferryland, Newfoundland.

The Teulon, Manitoba, Legion donated this former church to the town for use as a museum.

Once a church, this building now houses the Teulon Branch.

Cool, clear water. In St. George, Ontario, the Legion maintains this artesian well for public use.

An endangered species, the Atlantic salmon is being replenished in this Legion-sponsored fish farm near Tignish, Prince Edward Island.

In Great Village, Nova Scotia, two members sit framed by a gigantic Union Jack, said to have flown at the driving of the last spike on Canada's transcontinental railway back in November 1885.

Legion golfers on the links in Kelowna, British Columbia.

A branch cabin in a rustic camp for seniors in southern British Columbia.

Legion Corner in Winnipeg's Seven Oaks Hospital.

The rewards of participation in the Campbell River, British Columbia, Salmon Derby.

Hailing from a family that has boasted a mother, father, brother, and seven children all in the Legion, George Wambolt of St. Peter's, Nova Scotia, displays some 300 regimental badges donated to the RCL.

This Legion book depot in Montreal collects thousands of books to send to service people posted in remote locations.

8 *Legion Women*

Though The Royal Canadian Legion began life as a largely masculine organization, it has grown to include thousands of dedicated women. There are an estimated 5,000–7,000 ex-servicewomen members, many of whom are veterans of World War II. They reflect the same diversity of background and occupation as the men, and from their ranks have come provincial command presidents, zone and district commanders, and many branch presidents. As the number of Legion women grows with the anticipated influx of associates, it is likely they will follow the same patterns they do in contemporary professional life and seek even higher Legion office in the years ahead.

But when one thinks of Legion ladies as a group, it is often the almost 100,000 members of the Ladies Auxiliaries who spring to mind. Encouraged by original Legion charter, the LAs have existed as long as the Legion itself, and are now represented in almost all its branches and in some provincial commands as well. As mothers, wives, widows, daughters, granddaughters, and nieces of Legionnaires and veterans, LA members may range in age from

teenagers to nonagenarians; they may be students, grandmothers, teachers, homemakers, businesswomen, and ex-service women. And they have a proud history. During World War II especially, they mounted an enormous effort sending parcels overseas to Canadian soldiers and prisoners of war. As the troops returned, the LAs spent long hours in railway stations waiting to give them a rousing welcome home.

From their beginnings in 1926, the LAs have never looked back. Today, many branches could simply not survive without the vital services and cohesive influence of their Ladies Auxiliaries. They are legendary fund-raisers, indefatigable organizers, and the very spirit of the Legion's commitment to public service. Their well-executed campaigns benefit both the Legion itself and a huge array of charitable and municipal organizations. Energetic LAs generously support their individual branches and make handsome donations to local community bodies such as the Red Cross or Cancer Society, hospitals, schools, special homes, scholarship funds, and cultural and athletic centres. Much of their work is directed toward senior citizens, and they also have a special maternal regard for Canada's young.

In addition to raising millions of philanthropic dollars a year, the LAs donate thousands of hours to comforting the sick and the elderly, fostering development of the young, delivering meals to shut-ins, and placing medical equipment, furniture, and

The original executive of the first Ladies Auxiliary formed in Ontario in 1926.

entertainment facilities in hospitals and group homes. They run blood banks and drop-in centres for young and old, provide emergency relief when disasters strike, and distribute gifts and food at Christmas. Fund-raising bazaars and lotteries, gala celebrations, and sit-down dinners for hundreds are their specialties. No challenge is too great for their organization and energy, and the Legion's renowned conviviality owes much to them.

Each November the LAS play a prominent role in Poppy Week, and their volunteer labour and enthusiastic manner helped raise the number of poppies circulated in 1984 to almost 12 million — one for every second person in our country. And at Dominion and provincial conventions, their attention to detail and managerial skills make these complex reunions run more smoothly, just as their co-ordinating spirit is a force of harmony within the Legion as a whole.

Though relatively few LA members are graduates of military training, they operate with a disciplined efficiency that would do the services proud. And they like a rousing parade, a brisk marching band, and the colour and pageantry of the Legion as well as the men. On the whole, though, their presence is an understated one, for if it is true that the Legion likes to go about things quietly, it is especially true of the LAS. They are the very essence of the Legion's preference for unobtrusive benevolence.

In a sense, the time-honoured term "Ladies Auxiliaries" is a misnomer. They may speak softly within the legion, but their vital and tireless services are an essential infrastructure. They are auxiliary in name alone.

As sovereign, Queen Elizabeth commands the allegiance of all Legion members and in 1960 assented to the addition of "Royal" to the Canadian Legion's official name.

Expert bingo players at Montreal's Vetville handle several cards at a time.

A Newfoundland member makes a point at the Winnipeg convention.

A big cheque form for a big donation to its local branch by the St. Peter's Ladies Auxiliary.

Young women helping out during the papal tour.

Two LA members pitch in for a banquet in the Woodstock, New Brunswick, Branch.

A Legion member from an RCL post in California attends Dominion Convention.

Legion dress then and now, displayed by a member from Calgary.

Each year LA members spend thousands of hours visiting the sick and the elderly.

A service officer chats with a group of seniors watching a summer parade.

Veterans of World War II examine a Winnipeg monument to army, navy, and airforce service women of the Second World War.

Though well into her nineties, this lady is still an active member of a Nova Scotia LA.

A distinguished Legion member watches the Vera Lynn
concert staged in Toronto, 1984. Typically, the Legion
brought in disabled people to see the show.

This Legion meals-on-wheels team delivers hot food to shut-ins in the Far North.

Ladies Auxiliary members at a commemorative service in New Brunswick.

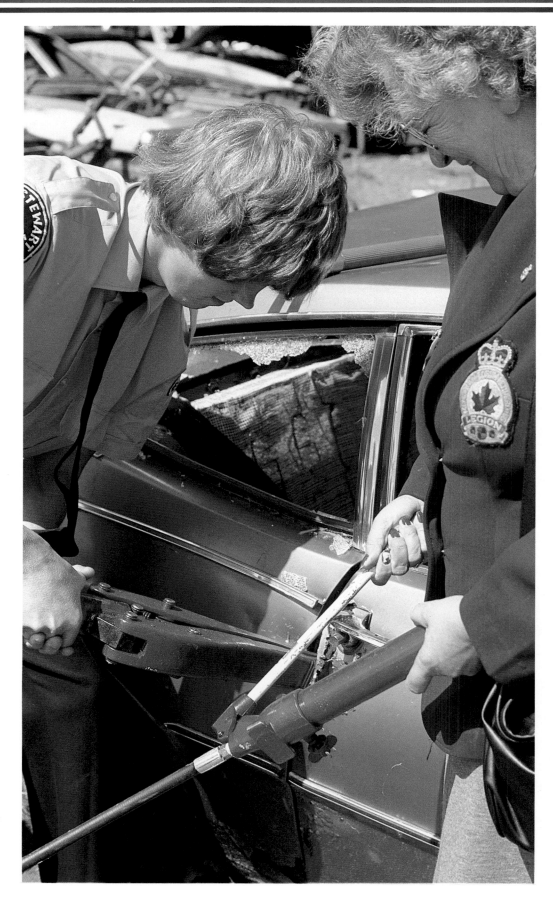

A Legionnaire from Prince Edward Island demonstrates the use of a set of the "jaws of life," a hydraulic apparatus for rescuing people trapped in damaged vehicles. Her branch donated the device to its local fire department.

Silver Cross mother Rose Ofredy responds to a toast at
an annual Valentine's banquet in an Ontario branch.

9 Old and Young

Out of the Legion's earliest championship of veterans' rights evolved its many-faceted Seniors Program of today. As the veteran population aged, the Legion's concern with its changing needs translated itself into an enlightened interest in Canada's elderly in general, a concern that government and social agencies would do well to imitate.

The current far-reaching programme penetrates every tier of the organization, from the smallest branch to Dominion Command, though, typically, its highest visibility has been at the local level. One outstanding development has been the building of thousands of self-contained low-cost housing units for seniors, often with progressive entertainment facilities and easy access for the disabled. Another forward-looking plan is the Geriatric Medicine Fellowship Program, providing annual bursaries for Canadian doctors and nurses who wish to do postgraduate study in the care of the aging and aged.

In addition, the Legion works in concert with the Department of Veterans Affairs to improve its Aging Veterans Program, which provides domestic and groundskeeping

A young air cadet with a senior Legionnaire in Ontario. The RCL sponsors hundreds of cadet groups across Canada.

The long jump at a provincial track and field meet.

Overleaf: A young lad inspects wreaths laid at the National War Memorial on Remembrance Day.

This little schoolgirl holds replicas of the scarlet tulips especially developed in Holland for the Diamond Jubilee.

assistance to qualifying veterans so they can live as long as possible in their own homes. It also continues to press for improvements to pension and war allowance rates and to insist on fair and efficient administration. It trains a watchful eye on all government benefits accorded the senior-citizen population, and in doing so enhances the prospects of all seniors, both veterans and civilians alike.

In keeping with this broader view, the Legion has membership in two Canadian gerontology associations, which promote the general well-being of the aged population. And a Legion representative sits on the national Secretariat for Fitness in the Third Age, a progressive non-government organization that urges seniors to stay young by keeping active and involved.

The message to its 1,800 branches has been well heeded, if we judge by the local programmes. Though the entirety defies cataloguing here, here are some of the developments: counselling for retirement; letter carrier alert; telephone reassurance

Top right: Legion-sponsored Brownies at a memorial parade in Lynden, Ontario.
Bottom right: An RCL sports official distributes trophies to young ball players in Welland, Ontario.

This rodeo queen was
sponsored by the Leduc,
Alberta, Legion.

A friendly briefing for new arrivals at the 1984 Dominion Track and Field Camp in Halifax.

In kilts and scarlet tunics, youthful members of a Legion pipe band march through the streets of a Nova Scotia town.

Clearing the bar at an RCL
track competition.

"On your mark, get set ... go!" A Legion official starts a race at a track meet.

Two Legion housing projects for senior citizens: Burk's Falls (top) and Montreal (bottom).

programme; both meals-on-wheels and wheels-to-meals plans; drop-in centres; publications for seniors; improved access to buildings for the disabled; vial-of-life medical information programme; home and hospital visits; transportation services; and sports and recreational facilities for seniors.

These programmes are enlightened ones and sociologically progressive, for it is estimated that over the next 50 years the percentage of Canada's citizenry over the age of 65 will rise to 18.3 from 9.5. In this context the Legion's move to improve the outlook for seniors takes on new importance. And it is a goal that will ultimately benefit all of us.

At the other end of the age spectrum is Canada's youth. Remembering, perhaps, their own young days in military service, Legionnaires have a special interest in the young. This regard first surfaced long ago in deeply humanitarian programmes like Jack Moore's Foster Fathers Group, which shouldered responsibility for the fatherless sons of servicemen killed in World War I.

Later it emerged in the Dominion Convention's 1956 decision to lend financial support to the Canadian Olympic Training Plan, a scheme to develop Canada's promising track and field talent to world-class standards. Then, in the early 1960s, The Royal Canadian Legion Sports Training Plan came into being. Under the direction of former British national coach Geoffrey Dyson 1,100 Canadian coaches were trained, who in turn passed on their skills to 60,000 young athletes.

Today the Legion's Dominion Track and Field Committee organizes an annual national track and field camp that brings several hundred promising young athletes together for rigorous training and competition each summer in a different part of the land. Most provincial commands also sponsor track and field competitions, and the Legion can take a little extra pride in the splendid

Overleaf: Warming to the music at a Quebec branch celebration.

135

A youngster raises dust for his RCL team at a summer baseball game.

showing of Canadian athletes at the 1984 Olympics in Los Angeles.

But its interest in sports and physical excellence does not stop at track and field. For it throws its weight behind thousands of minor-league teams from midget girls' softball to senior boys' hockey. The Legion's dedication to youth athletics is evident from the branch to the national level. It is also our largest supporter of Air, Sea, and Army Cadets and our major promoter of Scouts, Cubs, Guides, Brownies, and Pathfinders.

Two Legionnaires of different generations meet at the horseshoe pitch in Alberta.

Though team spirit and physical excellence are prime concerns, the Legion is also a staunch proponent of individual achievement and intellectual accomplishment. Proof is its wide sponsorship of local and national poetry and essay competitions, public-speaking and poster contests, and its generous bursaries and scholarships to thousands of promising young students.

In an even wider context, the Legion has also recognized the destructive social pressures that bear on the young in the modern

As the leaves begin to turn, seniors enjoy a Legion walk in the countryside.

age. It has sought to counteract them by providing positive role models and social and recreational alternatives to negative outlets for the frustrations of the troubled young.

These two segments of the population, the elderly and the young, reflect two different faces of the Legion, for it is itself both old and young. It is a mature organization that has undergone as many profound changes in its 60 years as any individual passing from birth to his sixth decade. It has more than a past, it has a history. But in the long-term scheme of things, it is still very young, and anticipates a long and fruitful life to come.

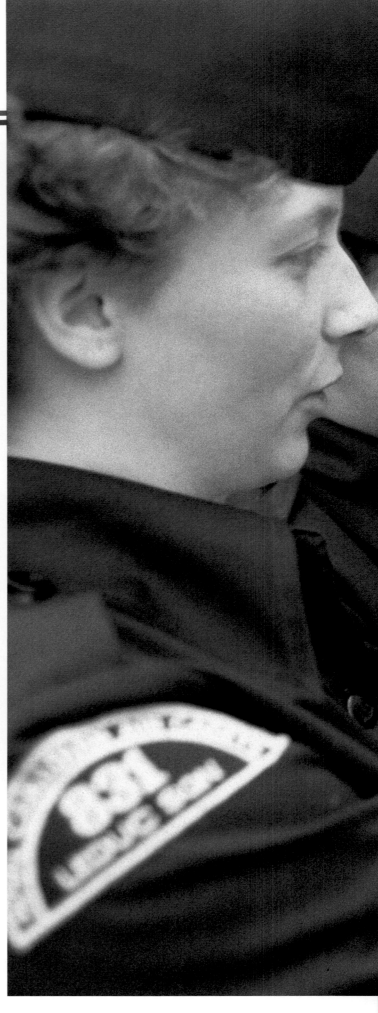

Top: Young sports camp medallists, Halifax 1984.
Above: Army cadets from New Brunswick examine a boot left over from World War II.

Alberta air cadets look over an illustration of a glider used in an RCL-sponsored flight training program.

Two young players await their turn at bat at a Legion game.

A senior citizen waters his garden in a Red Deer residence.

This graceful RCL clapboard house is home to elderly men in New Brunswick.

A songfest for seniors in London, Ontario, features hits
of the Blitz.

Legion coaches encouraging
young lacrosse players
in Esquimalt, British
Columbia.

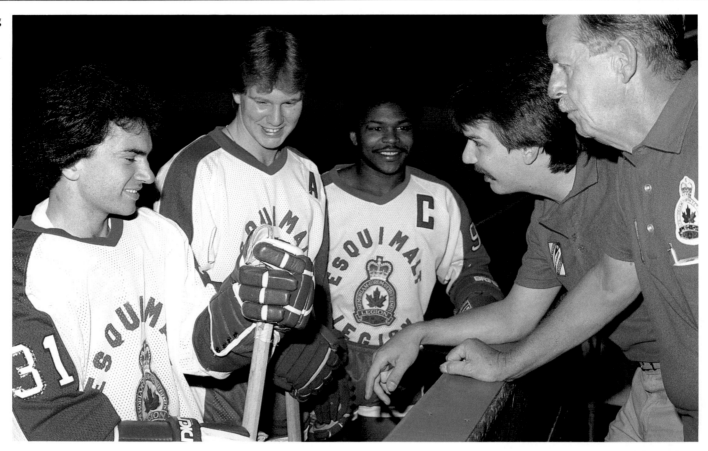

RCL members spruce up
the home of an amputee in
North Bay, Ontario.

Previous page: Athletes
strain toward the finish
line at the Ontario
track championships in
Burlington, Ontario, 1984.

"Keep moving, stay off the ropes, and watch out for his left hook."

149

A Legionnaire guides children through a mineralogical display in an RCL-assisted science museum in Sudbury, Ontario.

A bedroom in a specially equipped home for handicapped children, built by the Legion in Calgary.

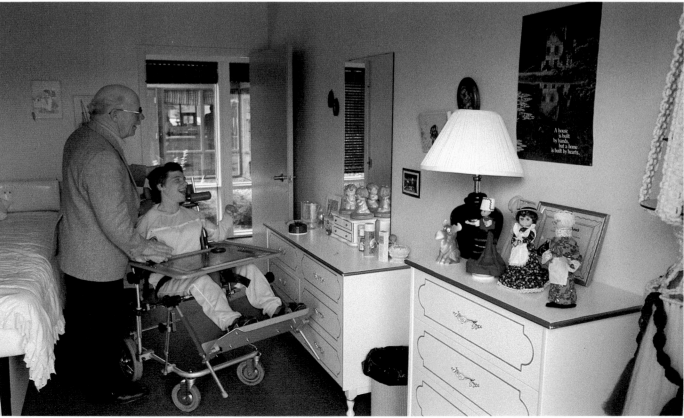

Dominated by a large fireplace, this is the livingroom in
the Calgary group home.

Overleaf: Though deaf and mute, this Maritime teenager
is being prepared by the Legion for a university education.
Here she takes a riding lesson with a Legion instructor.

151

In Rustico, Prince Edward Island, the winner of the first Legion essay contest coaches a young entrant in a recent competition.

A veteran member adjusts the lanyard of a young sea
cadet in the Maritimes.

Epilogue

It has been a long journey from the Legion's birth as a small, largely British veterans' organization after World War I to its present diversity and size. Membership now reaches into 2.4 per cent of our population, and through comprehensive community programmes the Legion touches many more Canadians. And by its continuing participation in world veterans' organizations, the Legion's influence is truly international in scope.

It has been a long journey, too, from the organization's early concentration on veterans' affairs and the rightful recognition of their sacrifices, to a broader involvement in national issues and social service. And it is an odyssey that has seen the Legion grow in response to the major events of the century: armed conflicts and cold war, depressions and recessions, waves of immigration, inflation, and profound social change. Though it will never lose sight of its concern for the fair treatment of Canada's veterans, who gave a large part of their youth in the service of their country, the Legion operates today as one of the most active community service clubs in the land.

And now, in its Diamond Jubilee year, The Royal Canadian Legion is facing perhaps its greatest challenge: the preservation of its large numbers and historic ideals in the decades to come. As the great armed conflicts of the century slip further into history, so, inevitably, does an increasing part of the Legion's traditional veteran membership. Today's leaders recognize that they must prepare to pass the Legion testament on to a new corps, one that draws heavily on the associate members who were granted full voting status in 1982. This is not a new or unique problem. A similar turning point faced the veteran leaders of World War I who placed the Legion mantle on the shoulders of the young ex-servicemen of World War II. And it is a shift that is similarly challenging sister organizations such as the British and American legions and the Commonwealth ex-services leagues.

To smooth this inevitable transfer, the Legion has redrafted its fundamental articles of faith, the principles that have served it for 60 years and that also guided its parent organizations, the Great War Veterans Association and the other fine ex-service associations that merged their identities to create the original Canadian Legion in 1925. This new document, it is hoped, will serve as a continuous bridge of commitment, reaching back into the Legion's proud past and leading the new generation of standard bearers into a confident future.

Legion members brave the rain and chill of November 11 to pay their respects at the National Remembrance Day service, co-ordinated each year by the Legion.

Articles of Faith

Whereas The Royal Canadian Legion was founded upon principles which endure today and will serve well all who belong or may belong in the future, including, among others: a solemn remembrance of Canadians who gave their lives so that our nation might be free; loyalty to the Sovereign and to Canada; safeguarding the rights and interests of the disabled, the widows and dependants and all who served; maintaining our right to encourage our people and nation to every reasonable support to peace at home and throughout the world; maintaining in and for Canada the rule of law, encouraging the national and united spirit and ordered government, and striving for peace, goodwill, and friendship between Canadians and among all nations; advocating the maintenance in and by Canada of adequate defences; retaining the spirit of comradeship forged in wartime and nurtured in peacetime to the benefit of the history and unity of the nation;

And whereas throughout the history of the Legion certain values have endured to the benefit of the veteran segment, the Ladies Auxiliary, and their chosen successors, all to the credit and benefit of the Canadian community;

And whereas it is the recognized duty of each segment, the one to the other, to perpetuate The Royal Canadian Legion and its principles, facilities, and programs for the general welfare of our nation now and in the future;

We, the undersigned, for ourselves and representative of our segment of The Royal Canadian Legion, covenant and renew our obligations to each other and to the nation and do solemnly declare:

Remembrance

That those who died in the service of the nation will always be appropriately remembered together with their widows and widowers. We will remember them.

That remembrance day shall remain and be reverently observed at the 11th hour of the 11th day of the 11th month of each year by us and our successors. Lest we forget.

That the sacrifice made by so many shall not be in vain and we shall strive to maintain unity in our nation, together with our constant endeavour to promote and maintain peace, goodwill, and friendship within our country and throughout the world, so that all citizens may be worthy of the sacrifice they made.

Just Rights

That those who survive and need our aid may be assured of reasonable and adequate assistance.

Loyalty

That we maintain our loyalty to the reigning Sovereign and to Canada and its people, to stand for ordered government in Canada and decline membership or to continue any membership to anyone who is a member of or affiliated with any group, party, or sect whose interests conflict with the avowed purposes of The Royal Canadian Legion or support any organization advocating the overthrow by force of organized government in Canada or encouraging or participating in subversive activity or propaganda.

Comradeship — Service

That our original basis of common service and sacrifice expressed in comradeship shall survive among us and our community so that the ideals for which so many laid down their lives will be fulfilled.

Membership
That The Royal Canadian Legion remain strong and united. That those who served or are serving or have served in the armed forces of our country together with their widows and dependants and such others as from time to time are admitted and subscribe and continue to subscribe to our purposes and objects, shall be encouraged to belong provided always that we shall remain democratic and non-sectarian and not affiliated to or connected directly or indirectly with any political party or organization. That so long as veterans remain, or their widows or widowers, that they shall be fully and adequately represented in all the councils of The Royal Canadian Legion. Future ex-service persons shall enjoy the same privileges in perpetuity.

Symbols
The poppy is our emblem of supreme sacrifice and must forever hold an honoured place in our hearts, an image immortalizing as it does our remembrance and honouring of those who laid down their lives for ideals which they, we and all Canadians rightfully cherish. It shall challenge us to serve in peace, as in war, to help those who need our help, and to protect those who need and deserve our protection. The cross of sacrifice, on appropriate occasions, is symbolic of the same worthy principles of remembrance.

The torch shall remain symbolic of justice, honour and freedom throughout our land. These were the principles for which our comrades fought and died. We of today and tomorrow covenant to hold it high lest we break faith with those who died. Justice, honour and freedom are our charge for now and forever. We serve best by fostering these principles in ourselves, our children and their children so long as The Royal Canadian Legion shall survive.

Our badge is symbolic of our loyalty to our Sovereign, our support to our nation in our worthy citizenship and our remembrance for our fallen comrades and fellow Canadians of like principles.

Our flag, being the Canadian flag, is representative of our nation both at home and abroad. We will uphold it ourselves and forever teach respect for it by our successors, within and without the Legion. At the same time, we will remember our historical association with the Union flag and the Red Ensign.

Our successors shall themselves learn and pass to their successors these principles including, when necessary, our best services in times of great need, our unique strengths to our family and community, and the worthiness of remembering their contributions in their continuing time.

We, individually and collectively, guarantee we will be true to these principles and, subject only to the limits prescribed by democratic law, teach and hand down them to our continuous successors without reduction but with enhanced values.

Postscript

This volume is a tribute to The Royal Canadian Legion in its 60th year. But long after the Diamond Jubilee celebrations are over, it will stand as a record, in images and words, of the Legion's progress over the past six decades. We also hope it will serve as an advance salute to the Legion's many and fruitful years to come. The book is intended, too, as a gesture of acknowledgment to Canada's citizen soldiers — taken in the broadest sense to include army, naval, and airforce personnel — who made great sacrifices to preserve the climate of life Canadians enjoy today.

The photographer and author hope to have done justice to the vitality and dynamism that have made the Legion a strong voice and influential force for 60 years. And we also wish to thank all the Legion people who gave so much time and energy to make the text and illustrations come together. We are grateful.

Telling the story of The Royal Canadian Legion was a great experience for both of us. And we wish all those who read this account a similarly satisfying one.

Diana Swift / Jack Jarvie
Toronto, April 1985

Trying her best at an RCL track and field meet, this youngster is typical of the Legion's long-term investment in Canada's youth.